# The A-Z of ghosts, skeletons and other HAUNTING horrors

**By Tracey Turner**

*Illustrated by Kate Sheppard*

■SCHOLASTIC

Scholastic Children's Books,
Commonwealth House, 1–19 New Oxford Street,
London WC1A 1NU, UK

A division of Scholastic Ltd
London ~ New York ~ Toronto ~ Sydney ~ Auckland
Mexico City ~ New Delhi ~ Hong Kong

Published in the UK by Scholastic Ltd, 2004

Text copyright © Tracey Turner 2004
Illustrations copyright © Kate Sheppard 2004

All rights reserved

ISBN 0 439 96326 5

Printed and bound by AIT Nørhaven A/S, Denmark

2 4 6 8 10 9 7 5 3 1

The right of Tracey Turner and Kate Sheppard to be identified
as the author and illustrator of this work respectively has been asserted by
them in accordance with the Copyright, Designs and Patents Act, 1988.

# Contents

# Introduction

Do you scare easily?

Maybe you pride yourself on being completely fearless?

Or perhaps you're pretty tough, but there are just one or two things that really give you the creeps?

However much of a scaredy-cat you are, everyone loves having fun being at least a little bit frightened. This is your guide to the world of ghosts, monsters and other assorted spooks, packed with fascinating but fearsome facts and ghastly things to do. So why not read on to discover:

• where to spot the world's scariest monsters;
• how to escape from a zombie;
• the best way to serve witches' fingers;
• a five-metre-tall, brain-sucking apeman;
• headless ghosts, poltergeists and a phantom house-brick.

This book is full of information you'll be glad you found out – some of it useful and some of it very strange indeed. Simply start at "A" and carry on until you get to "Z" (or the other way round if you'd rather), and you'll be ready to terrify the most fearless and fiendish of your friends.

## All Hallows' Eve

All Hallows' Day (or All Saints' Day) falls on 1
November. The day before, 31 October, is All
Hallows' Eve, better known as:

Halloween is everyone's favourite spooky time of
year, and has been for centuries... Long ago, the
Celts had a special harvest festival called Samhain
on 31 October. They believed it was a time when the
natural and the supernatural worlds became mixed
up, and ghosts and ghouls were out and about.

## Celebrate Halloween like an ancient Celt

- Start your Samhain celebrations at sunset on 31 October.

- Dress up in animal skins – the Druids (Celtic priests) did this as part of a fortune-telling ritual.

- The spirits of dead people will come back to their old homes tonight. Be sure to provide food for your ghostly guests – if you don't, they might bring bad luck.

- Leave out candles (perhaps in a hollowed-out turnip or beetroot) and food for any travelling ghosts.

- Make sure you don't do any crop gathering – the last day for this was 30 October and anything left now belongs to the fairies. Take it from them and you'll wish you hadn't!

- Sit around the Druids' enormous bonfire with the rest of your friends and neighbours and have a feast.

• Put out the fire in your hearth. Then take an ember from the Druids' bonfire and use it to relight your own fire – this will give you protection for the coming winter months.

### A Halloween tradition for butter-fingered spooks

German people hide their knives on Halloween night to avoid any nasty accidents with clumsy ghosts ... which is bad news if you want to carve your pumpkin.

### Halloween superstitions

*If you look into a well at 11 o'clock in the morning on 31 October, you will see your future. And if you listen to the wind at a crossroads, you'll hear about what will happen to you in the coming year. But never look at your shadow in the moonlight or you will be the next person to die!*

# B

## Banshee

In Irish folklore, seeing or hearing a banshee is very bad luck indeed. A banshee is a fairy woman whose appearance beneath your window – complete with horrible wailing cry – is a sure sign that someone in your family is about to die.

### What to do if you meet a banshee

Unfortunately, there's nothing much you can do, except hope that really it's Mrs Ramsbottom from number 42 calling her cat in.

here... puss, puss

## Bats

People often think bats are spooky – probably because of their habit of flitting about in the dark, and the fact that vampire bats are quite partial to feasting on blood. But in fact bats are fascinating creatures...

## Batty facts

• Vampire bats live on the blood of large animals ...
like you! They bite into the skin to make a wound
and then lap up the blood. They have special
chemicals in their saliva which stop blood from
clotting, and also stop the wound from being
painful – at least until after the bat has finished
with it. But don't worry too much: unless you live in
South America you're unlikely to come across one,
and vampire bats are much more likely to feed on
cows or other farm animals than on you.

• There's a myth that bats often get tangled up in
people's hair, but it's not true. Bats find their way
about using very clever echolocation and are
incredibly good at not bumping into things.

• Bats are your distant cousins. The bones in
their wings are just the same as
the ones in your arm and hand.

• Most bats live on insects
or fruit, not blood. They
might have become associated
with Halloween because
they swoop about near
Halloween bonfires, trying
to catch night-time insects.

## Bogeyman

The bogeyman usually lives under the bed. A terrifying creature, he is all the very worst things imaginable: he might have bat-like wings, sharp pointy teeth, huge claws, snot oozing from every pore and a personal hygiene problem. (At least, that's what mine's like.) Thankfully, all you need to drive him away is to stop believing he's there ... which is easier said than done, especially when adults are constantly pointing out that "the bogeyman will get you".

# Curses

A curse is a wish for evil or harm, which is supposed to come true if it's made by a supernatural being. In fairy tales, witches are fond of cursing babies at their christenings. But there are tales of terrible curses which many people believe. Here are two of the most famous ones – see whether you think they are true, or just a load of superstitious nonsense:

### The curse of the mummy's tomb

In 1922, the tomb of the Egyptian Pharoah Tutankhamun was opened for the first time by archaeologist Howard Carter. The tomb, which had lain undisturbed for many thousands of years, contained fantastic treasures buried with the dead king.

Rumour went that Howard Carter had discovered an inscription carved into the stone entrance to the tomb: *Death shall come on swift wings to him who disturbs the peace of the King.* The mummy's curse!

A few months after the tomb was opened, Lord Carnarvon – the man who had given the money to finance the project – died of a mysterious illness which might have been due to an insect bite on his cheek. Strangely, when Tutankhamun's mummy was unwrapped, there was a wound on the cheek – in exactly the same place as Lord Carnarvon's insect bite! Just seven years later, 11 people connected with the tomb's discovery had died of unnatural causes.

What do you think of Tutankhamun's curse? There were lots of people involved with the discovery – perhaps 11 isn't such a big number. Howard Carter himself didn't seem to suffer any bad luck. And maybe journalists at the time saw that a story about a mummy's curse was bound to sell newspapers, and so exaggerated things.

## The curse of *Macbeth*

Shakespeare's famous play, *Macbeth*, has been popular for nearly 400 years. It's a spooky story of murder, ambition and revenge, with a good helping of the supernatural in the form of three witches. But actors believe the play to be cursed...

The story goes that Shakespeare used *real* witches' spells in the lines he gave to his three witch characters, bringing a curse of bad luck on the play (see page 87 for some of the witches' lines). In order to try and avoid the curse, actors never call *Macbeth* by name – instead they refer to it as "the Scottish play". If anyone does slip up and say the real name of the play, he or she has to go outside, turn around three times, spit, quote a line from a different Shakespeare play, then knock on the door three times and ask to be let back in.

But despite actors' efforts to stop the curse, many strange and terrible things have happened at productions of *Macbeth*:

- Just before the first-ever performance of the play, in 1606, the boy actor due to star as Lady Macbeth died suddenly.
- In the play, Macbeth kills the king with a dagger. In 1672, the actor playing Macbeth used a real dagger and actually killed the actor playing the king!
- In one 1942 production, three of the actors and the costume and set designer all died.
- In 1949, a riot in a theatre where *Macbeth* was staged caused the deaths of 31 people.

And there are many more stories– a variety of bad luck has followed actors, designers, producers and directors of the play throughout its history.

Do you believe in the curse? Or maybe you think that any play might have its fair share of bad luck over the course of 400 years – it's a long time, and an awful lot of performances, so it's no wonder a few unfortunate things have happened. Also, there's a lot of action in the play, quite a lot of it on a darkened stage, which might explain some of the accidents. Is there a curse, or are actors all crackers? You decide.

# Day of the Dead

The Day of the Dead is the Mexican version of Halloween, and has its roots in an old Aztec celebration. It's a huge festival, lasting two or three days. Families decorate the graves of their relatives with lots of brightly coloured flowers and leave out offerings of food and drink. Then they gather by the graveside and have an enormous picnic, remembering their dead family members and telling stories about them. It's a happy occasion, despite the fact that there are images of death all over the place – plastic and papier mâché skeletons, skulls, coffins and gravestones are given as small gifts to mark the holiday.

To Great Grandpa

## Fearful food

Some of the food prepared for the Day of the Dead follows the death theme too – "bread of the dead" is baked with a bone pattern on the top and a plastic skeleton inside (it's good luck for the person who gets the piece with the skeleton), and "sugar skulls" are as big a part of this holiday as mince pies are for us at Christmas.

Impress the guests at your own Day of the Dead celebration (otherwise known as a Halloween party) with this Mexican recipe for ghoulish goodies. It's probably the most unhealthy snack you can eat.

## Sugar skulls

*Ingredients:*
200 g granulated sugar
1 teaspoon dried egg-white powder
1 tablespoon water
Ready-made icing in a dark colour, or add your own food colouring to white icing

*To make the skulls:*
**1** Mix the sugar and egg-white powder in a bowl.
**2** Sprinkle on the water and mix until the sugar mixture is damp – like the sort of sand you'd use for a sandcastle.

**3** On a baking sheet or other flat surface, shape the sugar into skull shapes – a bit like this:

**4** It's probably best if you keep them small, and no deeper than about 1 cm.

**5** Leave the skulls to dry for 24 hours, until they've hardened.

**6** Decorate with icing in a simple pattern – try this:

# Dracula

The character of Count Dracula was born in 1897 in a novel called *Dracula*, by Bram Stoker, one of the best horror stories of all time. In the book, the hero's business trip to Count Dracula's castle turns into a nightmare:

- he is attacked by three ghostly women;
- he is horrified to see his host, Count Dracula, turn into a bat;
- he discovers horrible bite marks on his own neck;
- he manages to escape

from the castle, only to find himself in the midst of a terrifying vampire hunt!

Dracula might be the most famous vampire, but vampires had been around long before he was invented (see page 82).

## Big bad Vlad

Bram Stoker took his character's name from a real person – he wasn't a vampire, but he certainly wasn't very nice...

Vlad Dracula became the ruler of Wallachia (now in Romania) in 1456. As ruler, Vlad was absolutely ruthless towards his enemies, or anyone who broke his rules. His favourite punishment was impalement, which meant his victims were speared with a stake, then hoisted upright. It was a horrible and slow way to die. While Vlad was in charge, many thousands of people were impaled for all sorts of crimes – even something as minor as telling a lie. Vlad also kept people in slavery, and had them burned alive, boiled, disembowelled or tortured. Some people were killed by Big Bad Vlad just because they were poor. There were even rumours that Vlad drank the blood of some of his victims. But impaling remained Vlad's favourite hobby, and after his death in battle in 1476 he became known as Vlad the Impaler.

## Elves

You might be wondering what elves are doing in a book about ghouls and ghosts. But in the folklore of Norway, Sweden, Finland and Denmark there are two types of elves: the goodies and the baddies.

The goodies are magical creatures that live in woods and skip about doing good. The baddies are magical creatures too, but they bring bad luck and ill health. They live underground, because daylight turns them to stone, so there's a good chance you'll never meet one...

## What to do if you meet an elf

Although you are unlikely to meet a bad elf in the daytime, if you should be about at night and spot a small, ugly creature, the best advice is to run away. On no account start a conversation with a bad elf – he is bound to outwit you and you'll probably end up giving him all your money or promising him something you'll wish you hadn't.

## Fairies

Like elves, you might
be surprised to see
fairies in a book of
spooks. But not all
fairies are like Tinkerbell in
*Peter Pan* – some are
dangerous spirits that are
fond of snatching away
young babies to fairyland and
exchanging them with
a supernatural creature
(known as a "changeling"),
whom you definitely
wouldn't want as a
little brother or sister.
Or they might lure you
into fairlyland, where
you could become
lost for ever.

### What to do if you meet a fairy

Fairies are likely to cause mischief, and so they are best avoided. Ways to do this include not going into the woods on your own (which is pretty good advice anyway), and wearing odd socks and inside-out clothes. (Of course, you also run the risk of looking like a loony.) If you do meet a fairy, try not to upset him or her. And if you meet the Queen of the Fairies, you have to say: "Hail to you, Queen Mab!"

### A scary fairy superstition

It's not a good idea to sit under a hawthorn tree on Halloween: if you do, you are in serious danger of being enchanted or carried away by fairies.

# Frankenstein's monster

People have been terrified by Mary Shelley's scary novel *Frankenstein* for nearly 200 years. In the book, the scientist Dr Victor Frankenstein experiments with bringing dead tissue back to life, and eventually he succeeds in making a man by using dead body parts. Sadly, it all goes horribly wrong: the poor

creature created by
Frankenstein is intelligent
and kind, but hideously ugly.
Dr Frankenstein is horrified
by his creation and abandons
him, and the creature
becomes a monster,
eaten up with hatred,
who eventually turns on
Dr Frankenstein himself.

## Frankenstein films

More than 40 films have been made about
Dr Frankenstein's monster, including:

- *Bride of Frankenstein*
- *Frankenstein Meets the Wolfman*
- *Frankenstein and the Monster From Hell*
- *Flesh for Frankenstein*

They sound nice, don't they? Sometimes people
call the monster "Frankenstein", but really
Frankenstein is the name of the scientist who made
the creature.

# Games

You can't have Halloween without playing some spooky games. Here are some you might want to try...

### Apple bobbing

Did you know that this traditional game probably comes from the ancient Romans? They had a festival around Halloween to honour the goddess of the harvest, Pomona, whose symbol was an apple.

*Players*: As many as can fit around your bowl

*You need*: At least one apple for each player; a big bowl (e.g. a washing-up bowl) full of water

*To play*:

1 Float the apples in the bowl of water.

2 Each player must try to get an apple out of the water without using his/her hands.

3 The first player to bite an apple and lift it out of the water is the winner.

> ### *Some apple superstitions*
> The winner of the apple-bobbing game is supposed to be the first to marry. In another apple game, everyone has to peel an apple from top to bottom; whoever gets the longest unbroken peel will live the longest. And if you throw the apple peel over your shoulder, the letter it forms will be one of the initials of your future wife or husband!

## What's in the bag?

*Players*: Any number

*You need*: Polythene bags; paper bags; peeled pieces of carrot, cooked spaghetti, small hard-boiled eggs or peeled grapes, mashed banana, cottage cheese, cooked rice

*To play*:

**1** To spectacularly spook your friends, put each of the items in a separate plastic bag and put each plastic bag inside a paper bag.

**2** Tell your friends that, earlier on, you dared to visit the local haunted house/graveyard, where you saw three weird-looking old women huddled round what looked like a big cooking pot. They were muttering an incantation and dropping things into the pot. You've brought back some of their strange and disgusting ingredients with you:

- maggots (cooked rice – you might want to add a few drops of vegetable oil for extra sliminess);
- dead men's fingers (carrots – it's amazing how horrible they feel);
- toads' innards (mashed banana);

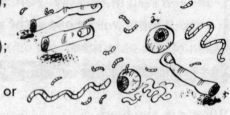

- eyeballs (small hard-boiled eggs, or peeled grapes);

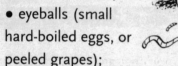

- worms (cooked spaghetti – again, some vegetable oil might add to the effect nicely);
- frogs' brains (cottage cheese).

**3** Pass round the bags and ask your friends to feel inside without looking. Ask them to guess what they're touching, then tell them the disgusting truth (don't tell them the real and much less disgusting truth until after everyone's been thoroughly freaked out).

You could also try the mummy game on page 52, the spooky quiz on page 64, or the trick-or-treat game on page 78.

# Ghosts

Do you believe in ghosts – the spirits of the dead returned to earth to haunt the living? If you do, then Halloween is supposed to be the time when you're most likely to meet one. Most of us would rather not meet a ghost, of course, and there are lots of charms to keep them away – here are some of them:

• A cross made from the wood of a rowan tree wards off ghosts, witches and other spooks. If the cross is bound together using red thread, it is supposed to be especially effective.

• Candles are supposed to protect against ghosts. But if the candle flame turns blue, it means there's one nearby!

• On Halloween, animal bones or a picture of a loved animal buried near the front door will stop ghosts from entering your home.

wooooohhh

- Ghosts and other spooks hate salt – sprinkle some about to keep them away.
- A broom placed across the doorstep will prevent evil spirits. In Eastern Europe, people would sometimes put brooms underneath their pillows ... which must have been a bit uncomfortable.
- To keep ghosts and ghouls at bay, you should walk anticlockwise around your home three times before sunset on Halloween ... and you have to do it backwards.

## The friendly ghost

Not all ghosts are something to be afraid of: take the Big Grey Man of Ben Macdui, for instance. Climbers in the Cairngorm Mountains in Scotland claim to have seen a three-metre-tall ghost known as the Big Grey Man, who watches over them until they reach safety.

For more ghastly ghostly information, see *Haunted houses* and *Poltergeists*.

# Ghouls

Ghouls are like vampires, but
they eat human flesh as well as
drinking blood (so never invite
one home for tea). They can't
stand daylight and like to live
near graveyards, as it's handy
for a continuous supply of
fresh dead bodies – a kind of
hideous fast-food outlet.

### *What to do if you meet a ghoul*

You will recognize a ghoul by its blue-grey skin,
pointed teeth, sharp claws, bulging eyes and thin
body. Since a ghoul will undoubtedly fall upon you
and start feasting on your flesh, the best advice is to
run away very fast indeed.

# Goblins

These small, ugly creatures, originally
from France, are responsible for
mischief-making in Europe and North
America. They sour milk, steal single

socks from the washing machine, and those sort of things. They have also been known to pinch naughty children! Not all goblins are a nuisance though: the mine-dwelling goblins known as Knockers are helpful to miners, as long as the miners make sure they're well fed.

### What to do in case of goblin infestation

If you have goblins in your home, you might like to try scattering seeds about – apparently goblins are very tidy creatures and this will annoy them so much that eventually they will leave. Of course, you'll probably end up with a mouse infestation instead.

# Halloween
See *All Hallows' Eve.*

# Haunted houses

In most neighbourhoods there's a building that's supposed to be haunted. And the more famous the building, the more famous, exciting and numerous the ghosts – or so it seems...

## The Tower of London, England

The Tower of London is supposed to be one of the most haunted places in the world. It's certainly true that hundreds of people have been imprisoned and executed here over the centuries. Its ghostly Hall of Fame includes:

- Ann Boleyn, the second wife of Henry VIII, whose headless body has been seen at the Tower since she was beheaded in 1536.
- Guy Fawkes, whose screams are said to echo through the building.
- The two princes, Edward and Richard, who have been haunting the Tower since they were murdered here as children in 1483.
- Sir Walter Raleigh, who was imprisoned here during the reign of Elizabeth I.

● Lady Jane Grey, the young woman who was Queen of England for just nine days before having her head cut off in 1554.

A phantom bear from the old Tower Menagerie has also been spotted!

## Glamis Castle, Tayside, Scotland

Said to be the most haunted castle in Britain, Glamis Castle is haunted by:

● King Malcolm II, who was murdered here in 1018.
● The White Lady, thought to be Lady Janet Douglas, who was imprisoned at the castle and burned as a witch in the sixteenth century.
● The ghost of Earl Beardie, who is said to be gambling with the Devil in a secret room in the castle.

I'll see you for three matchsticks

As well as Weirdie Beardie and his friends, there's also a Grey Lady, a servant boy, a tongueless woman and many more.

See *Poltergeists* for another haunted house.

## How to tell if your house is haunted

**1** Do you ever feel a chill down the back of your neck?

**2** Are there parts of your home that seem colder than others?

**3** Does your dog or cat ever growl or spit at something you can't see?

**4** Do you sometimes feel you are being watched?

**5** Do you ever hear strange cackling or wailing noises coming from empty rooms?

**6** Do ghost-hunters ask if they can spend the night in your house?

**7** Do objects move about on their own – sometimes flying across the room?

**8** Do you see transparent strangers walking through walls?

If you answered yes to more than three of these – particularly if one of them was number eight – your house is definitely haunted.

# Isnashi

The Isnashi is a monstrous ape-like creature of the Brazilian rainforest. Local legend says that the Isnashi used to be a man who wanted to live for ever, but ended up condemned to wander the forest as a tall, smelly, hairy, one-eyed beast. Reports of the Isnashi (which have, of course, never been proved) say that it is:

• five metres tall;

• disgustingly smelly – its odour is so foul that the creature is followed by swarms of flies;

• covered in hair so incredibly thick that no spear or bullet can penetrate it;

• highly dangerous – it is fond of twisting off people's skulls and sucking out their brains!

If you ever find yourself on the banks of the Araguaia River in Brazil, remember to keep an eye out for it.

# Jack-o'-lantern

An old Irish legend is the reason we carve pumpkins at Halloween. There are different versions of the tale – here is one of them...

### Jack and the Devil

Jack was a mean, thieving, drunken old misery-guts. One day, the Devil himself came to take Jack's soul. But Jack was wily, and managed to trick the Devil into climbing a tree. The second the Devil was in the branches, Jack put crosses all around the tree so that he couldn't get down again (because the Devil can't go past the sign of the cross).

Eventually, the Devil struck a bargain with Jack: if Jack removed the crosses, the Devil promised that he would never, ever take Jack's soul.

Years later, mean old Jack died. When he arrived at Heaven's gates, he was sent straight down to Hell, because he'd led such a bad life. But when he got there, the Devil wouldn't let him in because of his promise and sent Jack on his way, throwing after him a piece of coal from the fiery pit of Hell. So Jack was doomed to walk the earth for eternity, carrying the coal in a hollowed-out turnip to light his way, looking for someone he could trick into swapping their soul for his.

On Halloween, the night when the veil between the living and the dead is weakest, you might see Jack and his lantern. If you leave a light burning in a hollow turnip – or nowadays a pumpkin – Jack will think you're another lost soul like him and he'll leave you alone.

## How to make a jack-o'-lantern

Unless you want Jack after you, make sure you have your own jack-o'-lantern for Halloween. In the past, people have used turnips or potatoes, but pumpkins are easier and look prettier. Get an adult to carve it for you – pumpkins can be tough, and after all it's much better if *they* run the risk of cutting themselves.

*You need*:

A pumpkin; an adult with a sharp knife; a small candle or tea light

*To make the lantern*:

1 Get your adult to cut a big slice off the top of the pumpkin, including the stalk.

2 Hollow out the seeds and soft inside of the pumpkin with a spoon.

3 Draw your design for a spooky pumpkin face on the outside. (Best not to make this too complicated unless you have a very artistic and skilled adult.) You don't have to make it a face – stars and other simple shapes look good too.

4 Get your adult to carve out your design.

5 Finally, your adult should light the candle or tea light and put it inside the pumpkin, and replace the top.

# Jokes

You can't let 31 October go by without cracking some terrible spooky jokes. Here are a few you could tell – some of them are so awful, it's scary...

Why didn't the skeleton dance at the Halloween party?
*It had no body to dance with.*

Why do ghosts make bad liars?
*Because you can see right through them.*

Why might you carry a clock and a bird on Halloween?
*To go tick or tweeting.*

Why did the ghost cross the road?
*To get to the other side.*

What do you get if you cross a snowman with Dracula?
*Frostbite.*

42

**Stop!**

What do you get if you take the circumference of your jack-o'-lantern and divide it by its diameter?
*Pumpkin pi.*

What happens when a ghost gets lost in the fog?
*He's mist.*

What do you call serious rocks?
*Gravestones.*

Who was the most famous skeleton detective?
*Sherlock Bones.*

What did the bat say to the witch's hat?
*You go on ahead. I'll hang around for a while.*

What do you call a monster with no neck?
*The Lost Neck Monster.*

# Kappa

Kappa are particularly unpleasant creatures found near rivers in Japan. Their favourite hobby is luring people into the river in order to suck their blood.

### What to do if you meet a kappa

Although these creatures sound scary, dealing with them isn't too difficult: Kappas carry water on their heads that is the source of their magic powers. If you bow to a Kappa, it will be too polite not to bow back, spilling the water and losing its power. Another handy tip is that Kappas love cucumbers even more than the taste of your blood, so be sure to have one handy to bargain with.

## Living dead

See *Zombies*.

## Loch Ness Monster

The Loch Ness Monster – known to its friends as Nessie – has become Britain's most famous monster. The first record of a creature in Loch Ness, north-west Scotland, comes from a book written in 565, and since then hundreds of people (most of them in the twentieth century) claim to have seen a large, long-necked creature swimming in the loch.

Based on the descriptions, one theory is that the Loch Ness Monster is in fact a plesiosaur, a dinosaur that died out 70 million years ago.

None of the photographs of the monster is clear enough to be proof of Nessie's existence. The most famous photograph, of a creature a bit like a dinosaur swimming in the loch, has been proved to be a fake. Experiments with sonar (a kind of radar using sound waves) haven't revealed a monster living in the depths of the loch.

Many people continue to believe that Nessie lives in the deep waters of Loch Ness, and sightings of a creature are recorded every now and again. Perhaps people mistake driftwood or seals for a monster because that's what they want to believe. Or perhaps there really is something in the loch, hiding from the sonar in deep caves. Make up your own mind about the legendary monster of Loch Ness.

# Monsters

We've already met the bogeyman, Frankenstein's monster, a few ghouls and goblins, and the Loch Ness Monster, but of course there are many more. Here is a brief field guide to some of the most monstrous creatures said to be stalking various parts of the world today...

### The beast of Bodmin Moor
*Habitat*: Bodmin Moor, Cornwall. Similar creatures are reported to be roaming other parts of the British countryside
*Distinguishing features*: Big cat – like a puma
*Monstrous behaviour*: Attacking and killing sheep and other livestock; terrifying people

## Chupacabras

*Habitat*: Central and South America. Sightings continue to the present day

*Distinguishing features*: Long fangs, a spiked spine and red glowing eyes; human-like body

*Monstrous behaviour*: Feasting upon animals (its name literally means "goat sucker")

## Dover demon

*Habitat*: Dover, Massachusetts, USA, where it was spotted by separate independent witnesses in 1977. It has not been seen since

*Distinguishing features*: Big head, thin body with long fingers and toes, and huge, luminous eyes. A bit like Gollum but with orange eyes

*Monstrous behaviour*: Scampering about near roads; looking scary

## Kraken

*Habitat*: The high seas
There have been
reports of the Kraken,
or similar creatures,
ever since people first
went to sea
*Distinguishing features*:
Huge creature with long
tentacles – not unlike a giant squid
*Monstrous behaviour*: Overturning ships and
devouring the sailors inside

## Mokele mbembe

*Habitat*: The jungles of
central Africa. Sightings
of the creature (or
creatures) continue to
the present day
*Distinguishing features*:
The size of an elephant,
but with a long neck and
tail – like a dinosaur (some people believe that
dinosaurs never completely died out, and that this
region is their last remaining habitat)

*Monstrous behaviour*: Killing people who get too close – though the creature doesn't eat them, as it is a strict vegetarian

## Mothman
*Habitat*: West Virginia, USA. Several people have witnessed the creature, but it hasn't been spotted for nearly 40 years.
*Distinguishing features*: Headless, winged, man-like creature with glowing red eyes
*Monstrous behaviour*: Terrifying people by flying at incredible speeds past cars, peering in windows, etc

## Wendigo
*Habitat*: Canadian forests. In Native American myth, these creatures have been around for ever, and they're still being spotted today
*Distinguishing features*: Originally human, Wendigos can appear as three-metre-tall ice skeletons, or as tall, thin, ghost-like creatures

*Monstrous behaviour:* Killing and eating people, particularly children. Anyone bitten but not killed will turn into a Wendigo themselves

Other monsters you might spot in the wild include the Isnashi (page 38), the Ogopogo (page 54) and the Xueren (page 91).

# Mummies

The ancient Egyptians are perhaps most famous for their habit of taking dead bodies, pulling out the brains and the innards, preserving the bodies with chemicals and wrapping them in layers of cloth – otherwise known as making mummies.

They believed that only preserved bodies could expect to have another life after death. To us it all seems a bit scary, which is why mummies have inspired dozens of spooky films.

If you want to have a go at making your own mummy, try this simple game:

## Make a mummy

*Players*: At least four
*You need*: Loads of cheap loo rolls
*To play*:
**1** Pair up into teams of two: one is the mummy and the other is the mummy maker.
**2** Mummy makers wrap the toilet roll around their mummy until he or she is completely covered. No cheating – each leg and arm must be covered separately.
**3** The first pair to finish are the winners.

## Modern mummies

Did you know that in the last century Russian leader Vladimir Lenin and Argentinian first lady Eva Peron were both mummified?

# Nightmares

A nightmare is a
frightening dream
that wakes you up.
Sometimes it takes
you a while to realize
you've been asleep,
rather than falling off
a cliff, running away
from a flesh-eating
zombie or being
lowered gently into a
witch's cauldron.

Everyone has nightmares at some time. Ways of
avoiding them include not watching scary films or
reading ghost stories just before bedtime, and not
eating cheese in the evening. Despite what people
may tell you, nightmares *never* foretell the future: if
you dream about something horrible, it definitely
doesn't mean it's going to happen!

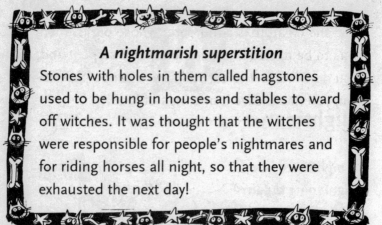

# Ogopogo

Canada has its own monster of the deep: Lake Okanagan in British Columbia is believed to be home to the Ogopogo, a huge, hump-backed monster which sounds rather similar to the Loch Ness Monster. Maybe they're related?

People who settled in the area around Lake Okanagan began spotting the monster in the 1870s, but the Native Americans knew about N'ha-a-itk, as they called it, long before. They had an ancient belief that the creature is a murderer whose punishment was to be turned into a terrible water serpent and, if you don't want it to eat you as you canoe past its lair, you must leave it offerings of food.

# P

## Parties

If you don't fancy the ancient Celtic Halloween celebrations on page 10, why not have a modern-day Halloween party instead?

## Setting the spooky scene

Try these party decoration tips:

● Lighting is very important in creating a spooky atmosphere. Make sure it's as dim as possible (without forcing everybody to stumble about shouting "ow!" every so often). See if you can buy some luminous glow-sticks and dot them about the room.

● Cut bat shapes from black cardboard and suspend them from the ceiling with Blu-tak and cotton. Do the same with plastic spiders.

● You might be able to persuade an adult to organize some dry ice for you – perhaps they could put it in a big cooking pot to look like a witch's cauldron.

● Jack-o'-lanterns are, of course, essential (see page 41).

• Make some paper streamers: take a long piece of paper about 10 cm wide, fold it into concertina squares, and draw a ghost, bat or pumpkin design on it, making sure the two folded edges are included in your design, like this one:

Then cut out your drawing, pull out the streamer and hang it up.

## Ghastly grub

You can't have food at a Halloween party without at least two offerings that look absolutely disgusting (but hopefully taste all right). Here are a couple of ideas:

### Bogies on a stick

*Ingredients*:
Bread sticks
Melted cheese (get an adult to do this for you)
Green food colouring
*To make the bogies*:

**1** Add the food colouring to the melted cheese and stir thoroughly.

**2** Dip one end of each breadstick into the green melted cheese, then stick it in a glass or other container, bogey-end upwards, to dry.

**3** Serve, explaining to your guests that the bogies are quite fresh.

## Witches' fingers

*Ingredients*:

Cooked frankfurters

Cream cheese

Red, green or yellow peppers

*To make the fingers*:

**1** Once the frankfurters are completely cold, cut off a small segment of each one like this:

**2** Spread the cut surface with cream cheese.

**3** Cut the pepper or peppers into fingernail-shaped pieces (it doesn't matter what colour they are) and stick them on top of the cream cheese.

**4** Make small cuts on the surface of the frankfurters for finger joints.

**5** Arrange tastefully on a plate. You might want to add some tomato sauce to the ends for that freshly chopped look.

Or you could invite your guests to sample a delicious cocktail...

## Dragon's blood

*Ingredients*:

Tomato juice

Worcestershire sauce

Salt and pepper

Sticks of celery

*To make the blood*:

**1** Pour the tomato juice into a glass.

**2** Add a tiny dash of Worcestershire sauce and a quick shake of salt and pepper.

**3** Put a stick of celery in the glass as a cocktail stirrer. Celery sticks also make good fangs, by the way – you'll need to cut them to size.

**4** If you want the cocktails to look really gruesome, add a stuffed olive on a cocktail stick to each glass (you can call these goblins' eyeballs).

### Radioactive green fizz

*Ingredients*:

Lime cordial

Lemonade

*To make the fizz*:

1 Half-fill each compartment in an ice-cube tray with lime cordial – you'll need a tray for each cocktail you want to make.

2 Leave it in the freezer for an hour or two, until it looks like green sludge but isn't frozen solid.

3 Scoop out the lime cordial and plop it into a glass.

4 Fill up the glass with lemonade.

5 Gasp as the lemonade becomes radioactive.

Punch (your favourite combination of fruit juices with some pieces of fruit floating in it) is simple to make and looks great if you serve it in a pumpkin punchbowl. You'll need to find a bowl that fits inside a big jack-o'-lantern.

You might want to look up some *Games* to play, *Jokes* to crack and spooky stories to tell at your Halloween party, too. And if you're going to dress up, look on page 75 for some easy costume ideas.

## Poltergeists

A poltergeist is a particularly troublesome ghost – one that throws things about and makes lots of noise. In the 1930s, one house became famous for its poltergeists...

## Borley Rectory, Suffolk, England

Borley Rectory was supposed to have had more than its fair share of ghosts: there was a nun, several headless men, a ghostly girl in white, and a phantom coach and horses galloping down the road outside.

All sorts of other terrifying poltergeist activity was reported too:

- Keys would shoot from locks, or lock people inside rooms.
- Bottles and other objects were thrown across rooms.
- Messages from beyond the grave were written mysteriously on the walls.
- Weird, unexplained noises were heard coming from empty rooms.

The house burned down in 1939, and the ruins were destroyed in 1944 – but not without a ghostly goodbye: in a photograph taken for *Life* magazine, a brick appears suspended in mid-air in a doorway.

The Reverend Foyster and his wife Marianne had lived in the Rectory and reported most of the ghostly experiences. Many years later, Marianne claimed that her husband had been responsible for the so-called poltergeists himself, because he wanted the publicity. But what about the brick? Sceptics claim that it was thrown by a workman and captured on camera by chance.

## Pumpkin

See *Jack-o'-lantern*.

# Quiz

Try this quiz on your friends and family, and separate the wizards from the wimps. If they score more than ten, they win a witch's finger, or as many bogies on a stick as they can eat.

**1 Which of these creatures would you expect to feed on human blood?**
**a)** Leprechaun
**b)** Witch
**c)** Vampire

**2 What is a baykok?**
**a)** Half-human, half-horse
**b)** An Icelandic wolf-like creature with a cry like a baby's wail
**c)** A supernatural Native American hunter with glowing red eyes

**3 Which of these is traditional on Halloween?**
**a)** Apple bobbing
**b)** Morris dancing
**c)** Fly-fishing

**4 What is a corrigan?**
**a)** A piece of ghost-hunting equipment
**b)** A Native American monster
**c)** A Celtic fairy

**5 Where do the lines "Double, double toil and trouble/Fire burn and cauldron bubble" come from?**
**a)** The Bible
**b)** Shakespeare's play *Macbeth*
**c)** Madonna's song lyrics

**6 In ancient Greek mythology, what is the minotaur?**
a) Half-human, half-dog
b) Half-cat, half-budgerigar
c) Half-human, half-bull

**7 What are the traditional colours of Halloween?**
a) Black and orange
b) Red, white and blue
c) Black and green

**8 What do you call a gathering of witches?**
a) A flock
b) A staff room
c) A coven

**9 Which of these might kill a vampire?**
a) A stake through the heart
b) A crossbow bolt
c) Steak and chips

**10 Where did the famous American witch trials take place?**
a) New York City
b) Salem
c) San Francisco

**11 Which feast day is the day after Halloween?**
a) Christmas Day
b) All Souls' Day
c) All Saints' Day

**12 The ancient Greek monsters known as Cyclops are famous for having...**
a) Only one eye
b) Only one leg
c) Two noses

**13 Which of these creatures usually lives under a bridge?**
a) A witch
b) A banshee
c) A troll

## 14 Where would you find the Ogopogo?
**a)** In the Scottish Highlands
**b)** In a South American jungle
**c)** In a Canadian lake

## 15 What is a bunyip?
**a)** A monstrous African bird that attacks zebra
**b)** A man-eating monster that lives in Australian rivers and swamps
**c)** Half-human, half-hamster

*Answers*

1 c) 2 c) 3 a) 4 c) 5 b) 6 c) 7 a) 8 c) 9 a) 10 b) 11 c) 12 a) 13 c) 14 c) 15 b)

# R

# Reincarnation

Some religions teach that although our bodies die, our "souls" come back to live again in new bodies. Sometimes people claim to have memories of a past life or lives...

### Jane's six lives

A Welsh woman called Jane Evans became famous because she claimed to remember six different past lives, which she could recall under hypnosis. One of them was a maid to a rich merchant in fifteenth-century France. Jane's story seemed especially convincing because she seemed to remember so many small details, all of which were perfectly correct. But Jane got one thing wrong: the fact that the merchant (called Monsieur Coeur) was married and had five children who all lived with him, while Jane said he was unmarried. It turned out that Jane's information came from a book about Monsier Coeur (which didn't mention the wife and kids), which she must have read and then forgotten about. The details were stored in her brain and came out when she was hypnotized.

No one seems to have found any real proof of reincarnation – it's up to you to decide what you think about it.

**S**

# Skeletons

Skeletons play a big part in Halloween celebrations. We find them scary because they remind us of death: after all, that's how we're all going to end up!

You might not think bones are particularly nice to look at, but they can be used as deathly decoration. Probably the most incredible example is at Sedlec in the Czech Republic, where human bones have been used to make the most unusual chapel interior. There's a bone altar, a huge bone coat of arms, and a chandelier that uses all 206 bones in the human body at least once. The bones are the remains of 40,000 people who were buried in the graveyard and then moved to make way for more burials.

### A scary skull superstition

*Drinking from the skull of a hanged man is supposed to cure all ills!*

# Spiders

Lots of people are terrified of spiders – the posh word for the fear is "arachnophobia". In fact spiders aren't all that frightening – OK, so they're not very pretty, but most of them can't hurt you.

### Spidery facts
• We should be grateful to spiders because they eat many of the insects that we find annoying or dangerous, like greenfly, mosquitoes and houseflies.

- There are about 40,000 different species of spider in the world. Only 30 of them have poison that can make humans ill.
- Baby spiders are called spiderlings. Cute, eh?

- The biggest spider in the world is the goliath spider, which can be as big as a dinner plate! But if one bit you, it wouldn't be serious.
- Spiders are very unlikely to be aggressive to humans – the only time they might be is when they're guarding their eggs.
- Spider silk is amazingly strong. Scientists are trying to find a way of making synthetic spider silk for use in bullet-proof vests – another reason to be grateful to our eight-legged, eight-eyed friends!

### A spidery superstition

*If you see a spider on Halloween, it just might be the ghost of a friend or relative. So make sure you don't step on it by mistake.*

### A strange spidery tradition

In India, Hindu wedding guests collect spiders to throw over the bride and groom – it's supposed to bring them happiness! Would being pelted with spiders make you happy?

# Trick or treat

Trick or treaters are the Autumn equivalent of carol singers – but this lot are likely to do something horrible if they don't get their goodies. The custom of trick or treating is most popular in North America, but in fact it all started in Britain from a number of different traditions:

• As part of the old Celtic Samhain celebrations, people would leave out food for the travelling spirits they thought were out and about at this spooky time of year.

• In England, on All Souls' Day, people would knock on doors asking for "soul cakes" in return for praying for the souls of dead relatives.
• An Irish tradition was for people to go door to door, collecting food for the feast of Saint Columba.
• Scottish children traditionally go guising, which involves asking for treats on Halloween night. The difference is that they're expected to do something (like singing a song or reciting a poem) in return for their treat!

The various traditions emigrated to America and became a way of letting off steam, with "tricks" like removing gates and boarding up windows! By the 1920s things got seriously out of hand, with adult trick or treaters vandalizing property. Thankfully, trick or treating has calmed down a bit now and the most serious trick to play on someone who doesn't give you a treat is to drape loo roll around their front garden, or spray shaving foam on their door.

## Spooky costumes

Of course, if you're going to go trick or treating it's compulsory to wear a silly Halloween costume. Here are a couple to try:

### The mummy

*You need*:
- Rolls and rolls of bandages
- Cold tea
- Safety pins

*To make the costume*:

1 Find out how many bandages you need to wrap yourself up completely, then soak them in the cold tea.

**2** After a few minutes they should look suitably old and unpleasant – take them out and leave them to dry.

**3** Wrap yourself up completely in the bandages – you'll need someone to help you with this – making sure you leave your eyes, nostrils and mouth uncovered! Secure with safety pins.

## The ghost

Here's a ghost costume that's a little bit more classy than an old sheet.

*You need*:

● Grey and white clothes – ones that look old-fashioned if possible

● Black, white and grey face paint

● Talcum powder or flour

*To make the costume:*

**1** Cover your hands and face (and any other bits of your skin that will be visible) in white face paint. Remember to add some shadows in grey and black under your eyes and between your fingers.

ooooohhh.

**2** Dress in the grey and white clothes.

**3** Sprinkle talc or flour all over yourself for a dusty effect – use some in your hair to make it look as grey and dusty as possible.

Accessorize your Halloween outfit with some fake blood. The simplest way to make it is to add red food colouring to syrup. The resulting sticky goo looks particularly effective, and tastes nice too.

## Troublesome trick or treating

If you can't be bothered with dressing up, going out and knocking on doors, get some counters, a die and some friends, and try this trick-or-treat game instead...

**1**

**2**

**3** A good start – go forward 4 squares to collect your first goodies.

**12** Your witch's hat blows off: go back 3 squares to retrieve it.

**11**

**10** Your trick or treaters run away while walking past the graveyard – go back to square 4 to get them.

**13**

**14**

**15** Mr Batty at number 46 won't give you a treat. Miss a turn to cover his hydrangea in toilet roll.

**24**

**23** You see a ghost! Miss a turn while you recover from the shock.

**22**

**25**

# WINNER!

I want my mummy

**4**

**5**

**6**

**9**

**8**

**7** You are too scared to knock at the door of the spookiest house. Go back 2 squares.

**16** The sweets you got at number 89 give you some extra energy – go forward 3 squares.

**17**

**18**

**21**

**20**

**19** You drop some of your goodies – go back to square 14 to pick them up.

help help help help

# Undead

See *Zombies*.

# Underworld

The Celtic underworld was called Avalon – a peaceful island that the Celts could look forward to after death. Different religions and cultures have different ideas about what the underworld is like:

• The gates to the ancient Greek underworld are guarded by a monstrous three-headed dog called Cerberus, who allows the dead to enter but never leave.

GRRRR

GGRRRR

Sorry mate, can't let you in without a tie.

• The ancient Egyptian underworld is a complicated place: its ruler is the green god Osiris, but there are lots of minor gods (including one with snakes slithering out of its cat's head), and various different levels and gates. Gate guardians have names like

Swallower of Sinners and Maggot Eater.

• Ah Puch is the Mayan ruler of the deepest level of the underworld. He is supposed to come up to earth looking for living victims to torture horribly.

• The Norse underworld is overlooked by a giant with the attractive name of Corpse Eater.

# Vampires

A vampire is a dead body that rises from its coffin at night and sucks blood from sleeping humans – which tends to kill them, or at least turn them into vampires, too.

### What to do if you meet a vampire

You'll know a vampire by its canine teeth, pale complexion, lack of reflection in a mirror, and – the real giveaway – the fact that it will be trying to bite your neck in the middle of the night. Although this sounds terrifying, there are various ways of dealing with a vampire:

- Vampires hate garlic – keep some about you ready to wave at them. They will flee from it.
- They will also flee from a crucifix, and they're not keen on any type of cross. If you don't have one handy, try making a cross shape with your fingers.

- Sunlight is death to a vampire: see if you can keep the vampire chatting till the sun comes up, then open the curtains with a flourish.
- The best method of dealing with a vampire is to hammer a stake through its heart. It's tricky, but very effective.

### A vampire superstition

*In Greece, people used to believe that red-headed people were vampires!*

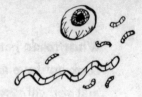

# Werewolves

People have believed in werewolves for hundreds of years. Werewolves look like normal human beings, but change into a wolf – or a cross between a human and a wolf – every full moon. In its altered state, the werewolf attacks people and animals; any person bitten by a werewolf will become a werewolf themself. In fact, there's a strange mental condition that makes sufferers believe they are wolves, so perhaps this is why people believe in werewolves.

ok take it it's yours

fido

### *What to do if you meet a werewolf*

Look out for signs that someone is a werewolf, so that you can be fully prepared when the moon is full. Hairy hands and feet (especially hairy palms), unusually long middle fingers, eyebrows that meet in the centre, and teeth that stick out are all dead giveaways. If you do end up meeting a werewolf, they are quite tricky to kill: you must use either a silver bullet or a knife made from a melted-down silver crucifix.

# Witches

Legend has it that Halloween is party night for witches, who gather together for a massive knees-up thrown by the Devil himself. Nowadays, no one believes in witches – apart from the modern-day kind who worship nature and cast spells involving different-coloured candles. But people used to think that witches were given magical powers by the Devil in return for doing his work, and lived among ordinary people. Witch-hunts began during the Middle Ages, with unfortunate people (mostly women) accused of witchcraft out of ignorance or spite.

## A cruel superstition

An old English superstition says that a witch's power can be destroyed by sticking pins in a pigeon or a stolen hen!

### How to meet a witch

If for some reason you want to meet a witch, wait till Halloween, put on your clothes inside out, walk backwards, and at midnight you should see one.

### A spooky spell

If you dress up as a witch on Halloween, why not add something extra spooky to your act and really freak out your parents? Memorize and recite these creepy lines said by Shakespeare's three witches in his play *Macbeth*:

Double, double toil and trouble;
Fire burn and cauldron bubble.
Fillet of a fenny snake,
In the cauldron boil and bake;
Eye of newt and toe of frog,
Wool of bat and tongue of dog,
Adder's fork and blind-worm's sting,
Lizard's leg and howlet's wing,
For a charm of powerful trouble,
Like a hell-broth boil and bubble.
Double, double toil and trouble;
Fire burn and cauldron bubble.
Cool it with a baboon's blood,
Then the charm is firm and good.

If you get a couple of your mates in on the act, it will be even better – make sure you huddle round a cauldron and drop things in at appropriate points. Afterwards, you could tell your audience that superstitious actors believe the words to be real witches' spells that have cursed productions of the play (see page 17).

# Wizards

The most famous wizards today are Harry Potter and Gandalf from *Lord of the Rings*. They're two of the most recent from a long line of fictional wizards that started with Merlin, the powerful and frightening wizard from the legend of King Arthur.

Stories about wizards are probably based on the ancient Celtic priests, called Druids, who were supposed to have had magic powers and the ability to foretell the future.

Why not grab a wizard's magic wand and perform some of your own magic?

## The magic number

*You need*:

- An envelope
- Some paper and pens
- An audience

*To perform the trick*:

**1** Take the year you're in, double the number and write it down on a piece of paper. So for 2004, write down 4008.

**2** Explain to your audience that you've made your prediction and put the piece of paper with the number on it into an envelope. Seal it in full view of the audience, or better still ask one of them to seal it for you and hang on to it.

**3** Pick a member of your audience and ask them to write down four numbers as follows:

- the year of their birth;
- the year of any important event of their life that they choose;
- their age;
- how many years it's been since the important event.

You might want to check they've got everything right.

**4** Ask them to add up the four numbers.

**5** Ask them to open the sealed envelope and read out your prediction: it will be the same as their answer!

**6** Bow gracefully as you are showered with applause, compliments, flowers, etc.

# Xueren

The Xueren is the Chinese version of the Yeti. This strange half-man, half-ape creature is over two metres tall, covered in brown hair and lives in remote forests. It is so fond of eating people that when it captures a human in its powerful grip, it faints with joy – but unfortunately it doesn't let go of its victim.

# Yeti

The Yeti is said to live in the tallest mountains in the world: the Himalayas. Sightings of the Yeti (also known as the Abominable Snowman) have been recorded since the nineteenth century, when a British army officer found enormous footprints in the snow, and in 1951 photographs were taken of a Yeti footprint. The Sherpa people who live in the Himalayas believe in the existence of the creature, and claim that it can make itself invisible. But the search continues: no real evidence of the Yeti has yet been found.

# Zombies

Zombies are dead people who have been brought back to life by supernatural powers. Since they're dead, zombies tend to have a blank stare, a greyish tinge to their skin, and they often have horrible gaping wounds or missing body parts. They have no will of their own, but carry out the orders of their masters.

### What to do if you meet a zombie

There's no point in trying to talk to a zombie as a means of distraction: if one is after you, there is nothing you can say to stop it.

The good news is that zombies are not known for their speed and agility: they shuffle forwards at a slow pace and have trouble with obstacles such as locked doors. These disadvantages should give you a good chance of escape.

Now that you know how to escape from a zombie (as well as how to dispense with vampires, ghouls, werewolves, etc.), you should be ready for almost anything.

# Also in the A–Z series...

*Find out:*

- how to build a snowman, stage a nativity play and other Christmas essentials

- the truth about sprouts

- some weird Christmas traditions you might want to try ... and a few you certainly won't

**IN THE SHOPS NOW!**